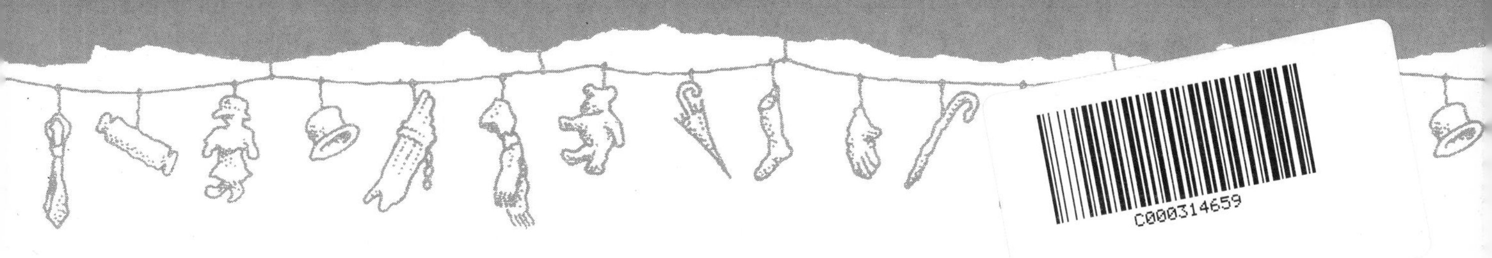

MOTHER SHIPTON'S
·PROPHECY BOOK·

The story of her life and her most famous prophecies

It is perhaps no coincidence that the voices of those who believe they see into the future are heard most often and remembered in times of great change. Our own time, approaching the end not only of a century but of a millennium, is such a one. So it was too when on a summer night in 1488 a young girl gave birth to an illegitimate child in a cave in North Yorkshire. It was not the first such child to be born – certainly not the last. But this child was to grow into a woman whose name still carries the mysterious power of prophecy. Why? What was it that made Ursula Sontheil, later the wife of an ordinary carpenter called Toby Shipton, so feared and respected not only in her home town of Knaresborough but throughout the land – and for centuries to come?

No one knows for certain the circumstances surrounding the birth of the child in a cave beside the River Nidd, on the other side of the river from the ancient castle of Knaresborough on its escarpment. For a century and a half everything known about the child who became Mother Shipton seems to have been passed on by word of mouth.

What is certain is that since 1641 there have been more than 50 different editions of books about Mother Shipton and her prophecies, some purporting to tell her life story in considerable detail. One of the earliest such accounts was said to have recorded the sayings of Mother Shipton as told to one Joanne Waller, who died soon afterwards at the great age of 94. That would mean Joanne, as a young girl, had listened to the old lady not long before her death in 1561.

Nevertheless all these various accounts have found some deep response in the public mind, just as they do today. It is easy to overlook the power of the spoken word, passed down from generation to generation, and to rely too much on written evidence. At the time when Ursula Sontheil was born few could read. Nor was there much to read: William Caxton had set up his printing press in London only 12 years before. Imagine the hunger for stories, for news, when there was no such means of communication and the only light when darkness fell was a flickering tallow candle, if you could afford it, or a rush stem dipped in fat.

So stories were passed on, sometimes embroidered a little. Like the story about the young nobleman who came to consult Mother Shipton and ask if she might foretell his father's death – preferably how soon. He needed money and if he could inherit his father's money he might escape his creditors. If she could tell him that the old man might die sooner rather than later, well at least he would be allowed a little time.

But Mother Shipton would say nothing to him. Then the young man himself became ill, and his father came to ask for an assurance that his son would recover. She answered him:

"Those who gape out for others' death
Their own, unlooked for, comes about.
Earth he did seek; ere long, he shall have
Of earth his fill; within his grave."

Soon afterwards the young man died. One of the servants told his father of the visit to Mother Shipton. Word went round of her power to foretell the future, perhaps to punish the wicked.

Tales like this increased the awe in which Mother Shipton was regarded. Even before her marriage, when she was a young girl, there were rumours of her powers to avenge unkind remarks, to play tricks on those who taunted her. "Witch" some would call her, or "Child of the Devil". She was probably physically malformed in some way, perhaps with a crooked spine or a hunch back. And her very intelligence may have made that deformity harder to bear.

Accounts of her birth all refer to her mother Agatha as an orphan, known to be "slothful and idle" – which may simply mean that she preferred casual prostitution rather than the hard grind of work in the fields or in some scullery kitchen. Word was that she was seduced by a handsome charmer who found her dreaming one day on a shady bank, and thereafter kept her in some comfort while he continued to visit her. It is said that one of the women who attended her in childbirth heard her say the young man's touch was "as cold as ice or snow". When she became pregnant outraged neighbours demanded that she should be prosecuted for incontinency – prostitution. She was taken before a local Justice.

At least she seems to have had courage. Although only 15 years old and "enormous with child", Agatha faced her accusers and clearly reminded the judge that he was in no position to complain about her condition – she happened to know that two of his own servant girls were with child by him at that very moment. Uproar in court: case dismissed.

When she went into labour it was in a shallow cave on the banks of the River Nidd. Close by was the ancient well with waters of mystical powers. Leave a shawl, a broken doll, perhaps even a body in that pool, beneath the trickling curtain of apparently clear water, and they would turn to stone. Even the leaves of the ivy that trailed in a dark curtain over its glistening canopy seemed to whiten and harden as you watched. And it was one of those stifling nights of July when thunder rumbles round the rim of darkness. On such nights are portents seen. The woman who came to help Agatha spoke of a smell of sulphor and a great crack of thunder as the child came into the world. And the baby, they said, was huge and misshapen. Even as it was being born it "jeered and laughed" and the storm was silenced.

Poor Agatha. Nevertheless it seems that whoever had hitherto supported her financially continued to do so. And it is curious that despite everything and indeed even in the face of local opposition, she was able to persuade a churchman of some eminence to baptise her child.

The Abbot of Beverley must have been some senior figure and indeed perhaps the head of the monastic foundation at Beverley, near Hull. Beverley has a beautiful minster church which might have been much admired even in Agatha Sontheil's time. And although it is some 60 miles away from Knaresborough the monastery held lands over a wide area. So was there a connection between this man, who put his own position in some jeopardy by baptising a baby girl whom some said was a Daughter of the Devil, and the child's mother?

Whatever her true parentage, little is known of the childhood of Ursula Sontheil. But it does appear that she was only about two years old when her mother gave her into the care of a foster mother. Agatha herself is said to have spent the rest of her life in a convent, possibly in Nottingham.

There is no doubt that Ursula was a bright and mischievous little girl. One of the first stories about her refers to the trouble she caused the woman who had agreed to look after her. Finding her front door open on returning from an errand, Ursula's foster mother feared she had been burgled and called her neighbours to join her as she nervously entered the house. They said afterwards that there had been dreadful wailing noises and that they had somehow been prevented by some invisible means from going into the kitchen. A passing clergyman calmed them down and led the way. The cradle was empty. Ursula, then aged about two, was discovered sitting naked on the iron bar in the chimney from which the cooking hooks were suspended. She was smiling happily, "very pleased at these pleasant exploits", so the account records. It was perhaps not inconceivable that her foster mother, fearing that someone might accuse her of leaving the child alone, should blame the Devil. And so the gossip spread.

Many accounts of Mother Shipton's early life make reference to her playing tricks on people. One such account in 1686 describes the kind of everyday torment she had to endure and the way in which she hit back.

"As our Ursula grew up to riper years, she was often affronted by reason of her deformity, but she never failed to be revenged on those that did it; as, one day, all the chief of the Parish being together at a merry meeting, she coming thither on an occasional errand, some of them abused her by calling her the Devil's bastard, and Hag-face, and the like..."

But as the worthy gentlemen of the Parish sat down to dinner after this unpleasant piece of ribaldry, strange events took place.

Mother Shipton's Cave entrance

The famous Petrifying Well.

"One of the principal yeoman, that thought himself spruce and fine, had in an instant his ruff (which is those days they wore) pulled off, and the seat of an house office clapped in its place; he that sat next to him, bursting out into laughter at the sight hereof, was served little better, for his hat was invisibly conveyed away, and the pan of a close-stool which stood in the next room, put on instead thereof."

An "house of office", it must be said, was a lavatory – and the "pan of a close-stool" was the chamber pot conveniently provided for the use of those taken short during dinner.

It all became rather ruder after that and there is a lot about "breaking of wind" and uproarious laughter, and the landlord of the inn appearing in the doorway to find out what was going on, and being discovered with a large pair of horns on his head. It is pretty certain that they regarded Ursula Sontheil with a good deal more respect after that. And you realise how she must have kept a sense of humour despite the loneliness she must so often have felt.

She must have longed for a husband, just as any other girl did, although her chances must have looked a trifle slim. Yet there was talk about her money – there always had been and you wonder whether Ursula herself perhaps encouraged it. It was said that she may have used a love-powder or some charm. But whatever means she used – and after all many men are suspicious of beauty when it comes to marriage – one Toby Shipton, a carpenter by trade, paid court to Ursula Sontheil. They were married in 1512, when she was 24.

The Petrifying Well from the River Nidd.

The times were momentous. Three years before, Henry VIII had been crowned the new King of England. He was still only 21, brave and handsome, a romantic figure who seemed to excel at everything, who could play the lute as well as he could ride a horse, yet who understood not only government but the hearts of the people. But among his advisors was Thomas Wolsey, son of an Ipswich butcher, and soon to become Archbishop of York and Cardinal of Rome. The seeds of turmoil were sown.

For Mother Shipton, now a respectable married woman, portents of the wider world must have been easier to ignore now that she had a more secure place in society. She and Toby did not, it seems, have any children but were "very comfortable" together.

It was only about a month after her marriage that one of her neighbours came to ask her help. Someone had stolen a new smock and petticoat. Clothes were expensive items in those days. A good linen smock alone would be worth a lot of money and would be expected to last for years. It must have been rather as if one of us had lost a rather special new dress for which we had paid more than we could afford.

Mother Shipton's reaction to her distraught neighbour was, you feel, rather characteristic. She roundly declared that she knew very well who had stolen the clothes and that she would make sure the thief returned them.

The following Market Day, as Mother Shipton predicted, she did. Through the crowds around the Market Cross in Knaresborough came a woman – wearing the stolen smock over her own dress with the petticoat in her hand. She approached Mother Shipton's neighbour, who, as directed, was waiting by the Cross. As she came she danced and sang:

"I stole my neighbour's smock and petticoat,
I am a thief and here I show it."

Then she gave the garments to their rightful owner, curtsied and departed – scarlet in the face with catcalls ringing in her ears.

It is more than likely that Mother Shipton did indeed know who had stolen the clothes and that she persuaded the thief to return them by using the threat of her mystical, perhaps Devilish powers. Her clever handling of events like this gave her a growing reputation. People began to believe her when she seemed to be foretelling the future, especially when her words were borne out by events:

"Water shall come over Ouze Bridge; and a windmill shall be set upon a tower, and an Elm Tree shall lie at every man's door..."

"Aha," people said, repeating these lines, when one of the local marvels of the day took place. York acquired a piped water system. The river was conducted through pipes laid across the bridge over the River Ouse and a windmill drew up the water. The pipes themselves were made of small tree trunks, bored out to make them hollow like pipes, and therein lies one of those small practical realities that add to the accumulation of tiny touchstones of truth in the story of Mother Shipton: the trees were elm and elm, unlike other woods, does not rot when immersed in water.

Then on another occasion, Mother Shipton remarked that her maid drove in a carriage over Trinity Steeple, and someone recorded her prophecy.

"Before Ouze Bridge and Trinity Church meet, what is built in the day shall fall in the night, till the highest stone of the Church be the lowest stone of the Bridge."

Not long afterwards the steeple of York's Trinity Church did fall: there was a tremendous storm one night and not only did the steeple crack but a good deal of the bridge was swept into the river by the floodwater. The bridge was rebuilt and, as part of its new foundations, the builders used the fallen stone from the top of Trinity Church steeple.

Mother Shipton does seem to have disliked pompous dignitaries and the Mayor of York was perhaps unwise to have crossed her in some way, for she was heard to comment:

Old Inn Sign at Knaresborough, over 200 years old, painted on Copper.

"When there is a Lord Mayor living in Minster-yard, let him beware of a stab."

A Lord Mayor did indeed come to live in the Minster Yard – one night he was mugged and died of three stab wounds.

Her reputation began to spread beyond Yorkshire. The world of great men began to touch her. It was not long after her marriage that she spoke about the King himself.

Henry VIII was a romantic – perhaps one reason why he had six wives. One of his heroes was his predecessor Henry V, who had so triumphantly defeated the French army at Agincourt. Enmity and rivalry between France and England had never really ceased. Encouraged by Thomas Wolsey, who had his own ambitious reasons for wanting the war, Henry decided to invade France.

Everyone in England knew about this decision. There might be no newspapers or television but everyone knew that there was, in effect, a national call-up. Henry had no standing army, no regular troops. So the King's men were sent throughout the country to find men to fight – to be drummed out of every shire.

Henry's campaign was not a success at first. But he did not give up and in 1513, with the help of Austrian mercenaries provided by the Emperor Maximilian, he won his "Battle of the Spurs" – said to be so-called because the French, taken unawares, ran away so fast. Perhaps it was said that the young King had won his spurs too. England celebrated a victory at last. Mother Shipton's words were understood:

"When the English Lion shall set his paw on the Gallic shore, then shall the Lilies begin to droop for fear; there shall be much weeping and wailing amongst the ladies of that country,

The Wishing Well

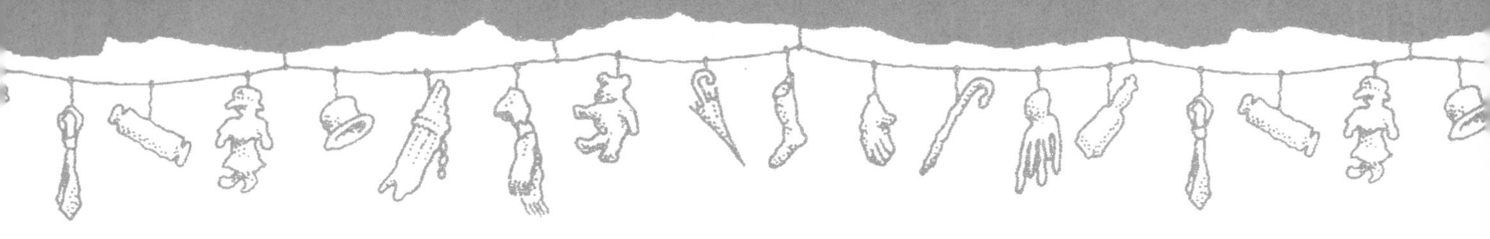

because the Princely Eagle shall join with the Lion to tread down all that shall oppose them. And though many Sagitaries shall appear in defence of the Lilies, yet shall they not prevail; because the dull Animal of the North shall put them to confusion."

Henry, of course, was the English Lion and the Lilies were the emblem of France. The Princely Eagle was Maximilian of Austria. The word "Sagitaries" refers to the French cavalry – think of the zodiac sign of Sagittarius, half-man, half-horse. The "dull Animal of the North" represents our own English soldiers, no doubt dragged out of inns and corners of the country, decidedly dull and grumbling about the weather, much as British soldiers always do.

Thomas Wolsey, who had encouraged Henry in his quest for glory, shared in the French triumph. He was only in his early 40s when, soon after the Battle of Spurs, he became Lord Chancellor of England and Cardinal of Rome – one the gift of the King, the other of the Pope. Wolsey wanted to be Pope and in the meantime he lived like a prince with a vast retinue of servants. He built a palace finer than any Henry himself possessed, Hampton Court, and founded Christ Church College, Oxford. Mother Shipton called him "the Mitred Peacock".

"Now shall the Mitred Peacock first begin to plume, whose Train shall make a great show in the World – for a time; but shall afterwards vanish away, and his great Honour come to nothing."

Cardinal Wolsey was also hated in the country. Even today the Chancellor is never the most popular man in government. He is responsible for taxes. In Henry's absence, Wolsey ruled England. Increasingly heavy and indiscriminate taxes were demanded and even the poorest people felt their effects.

Knaresborough Castle

Times were uneasy; there was hunger in the air again. Mother Shipton, in her remote home in Knaresborough, was as much or more aware of it than anyone. News came by word of mouth, passed on by travellers, by gossip in taverns and servants' halls, by pedlars and market traders. People began to want reassurance about the future and they came to Mother Shipton to find it. Richard Head, the Irish scholar who wrote one of the 17th century accounts of her life, described the widespread feeling:

"And, as the nature of English people is rather to desire to know what is to come, than to seek to rectify anything that is done amiss, so the greatest part of her visitants came only to be resolved of what she knew would come to pass."

One of these visitors was the Abbot of Beverley. He must have been by then an old man. Perhaps Wolsey's attacks on small monasteries to fund his own schemes had worried the Abbot, fearful for Beverley itself.

Mother Shipton said many things to the Abbot of Beverley about what might happen, and it is unlikely that this old man was reassured by her words. It is said that the manuscripts recording them were preserved "in a noble family" but no one knows which one; it is probable, however, that the Abbot was accompanied by a scribe who wrote down Mother Shipton's prophecies at the time.

She began to speak in images which he no doubt recognised as referring to the current controversy over Henry VIII's desire to have his first marriage to Catherine of Aragon annulled, so that he might marry Anne Boleyn. Anne Boleyn is the "Bull" of the prophecy, partly because of her name – then "Bulloigne" – and the black bull's head in her family crest. Henry, in whose coat of arms as Earl of Richmond appeared a cow, takes the female part – which is the kind of rude conceit enjoyed in the 16th century. The "lower shrubs" are the smaller monasteries, while the "great Trees" are those which were much larger and more prosperous.

"When the Cow doth ride the Bull,
Then, Priest, beware thy Skull;
And when the lower shrubs do fall,
The great Trees quickly follow shall.
The Mitred Peacock's lofty Pride
Shall to his Master be a guide,

St John's Parish Church and the Old Manor House

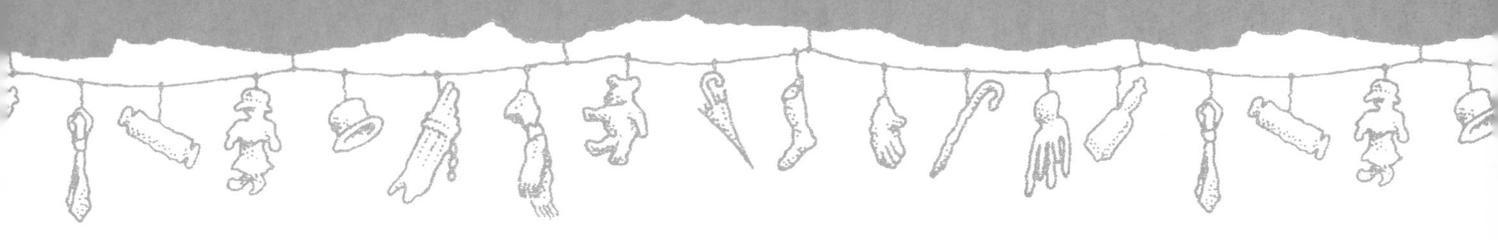

And one great Court to pass shall bring
What was never done by any king.
The Poor shall grieve, to see that day,
And who did feast, must fast and pray.
Fate so decreed their overthrow
Riches brought Pride, and Pride brought woe."

So Mother Shipton prophesied the Dissolution of the Monasteries, begun by the Mitred Peacock Cardinal Wolsey, and carried through by the king and his Parliament over the next 20 years. The Poor did indeed grieve. They lost their monastic schools, homes for the sick and destitute, the charities and alms so long given by and through the monastic foundations. As the wealth and land held by the monasteries were disposed of, they began to be resold to the emerging middle classes and existing noble families. There is nothing new about City speculators. They were at it in the middle of the 16th century, handling the resale and investment of land, property, grants and leases. The whole basis of land ownership that underpins modern Britain goes back to that change from religious to secular ownership of land, and its distribution among those who were best at grabbing a share.

But Mother Shipton had not finished with Cardinal Thomas Wolsey. It cannot have been long after the Abbot's first visit to her that she found someone else at her door. This time it was someone called Mr Beasley. She seems to have known him, but not his three companions and they did not give their real names. But she knew exactly who they were.

Knaresborough

Cardinal Wolsey had evidently heard about Mother Shipton's prophecies of his downfall. The latest was that he would never see the city of York – despite being its Archbishop. It must have made him uneasy. They were troubling times for Wolsey, in any case: he had not managed to pacify Henry over the matter of his marriage to Anne Boleyn, which the Pope refused to sanction. He was having a few sleepless nights. No doubt after one such dark night he despatched three lords to see Mother Shipton – and, with luck, to silence her. So the Duke of Suffolk, Charles Brandon, together with Lord D'Arcy from Yorkshire and the Earl of Northumberland, Lord Percy, approached the mysterious Mr Beasley in York and asked him to take them to Mother Shipton's house.

She was very welcoming, calling her maid to bring refreshments, inviting her callers to come and sit down by the great log fire. But Ursula Shipton was not only well aware who these gentlemen were, but why they had come.

"Mother Shipton," said Charles, Duke of Suffolk, "you would hardly make us so welcome if you knew what we had come about."

Ursula smiled and poured him another mug of ale. "There's no reason why the messenger should be hanged," she said lightly.

"Look – you know why we're here. You said the Cardinal should never see York. He doesn't like it."

"I didn't say he should never see York," she answered amiably. "I said he might see York – but never reach it."

"Well," the Duke said, uneasily, "he's saying that when he does come to York, you'll be burned at the stake."

"We shall see," said Ursula, and taking her married woman's kerchief from her head, she threw it into the fire. The flames licked around it. But it did not burn. Then she took the staff that she carried – probably because of a limp caused by her deformity – and threw that too on the fire. But it did not burn. She reached forward and took it out of the flames. "If this had burned," she said, "I might have too."

And she glanced at the Duke of Suffolk. In his eyes was the fear of witchcraft which lived inside every man. "My love," she called him. "The time will come when you will be as low as I am and that's a low one indeed."

Clifford's Tower York Castle

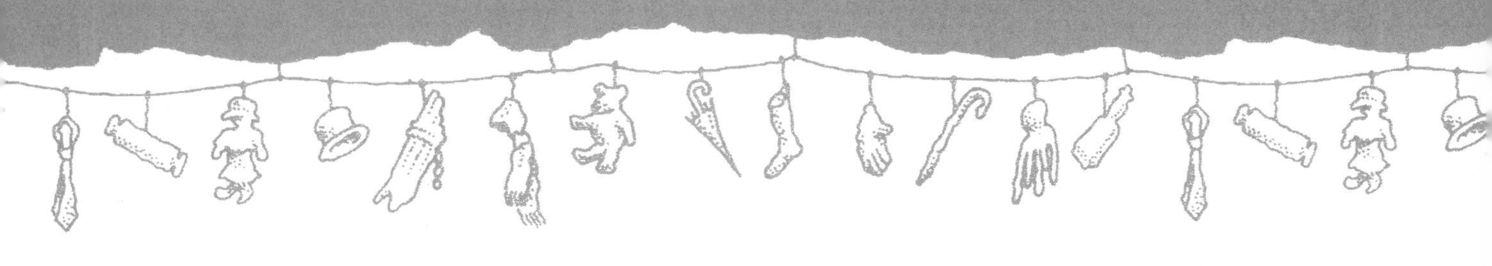

Riverside walk

Her voice was bitter. And when Lord D'Arcy and the Earl of Northumberland felt impelled to ask if she knew of their future they came away sombre, for she spoke of them being dead upon York pavements.

Some time after this meeting Cardinal Wolsey left London for York. It was a long, often dangerous journey. And his penultimate destination was Cawood, a village some ten miles to the south of the city.

You can still see a medieval tower, incorporated into an otherwise ordinary street in Cawood. This was Cawood Castle, seat of the Primates of the Northern Province of England – not, as it happens, York itself. Now Wolsey had come to find a kind of refuge in the place which, in the early years of his power, he had long neglected. He was already ill. But he could not resist climbing to the top of the tower to see if he could discern York in the distance. Perhaps, in the clear evening light, he believed he could.

1914 postcard

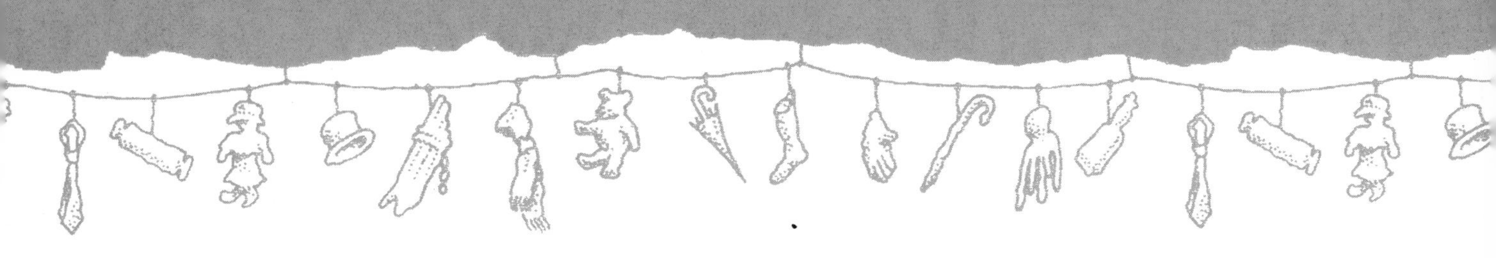

High Bridge, the main entrance

"Someone has said," he remarked, "that I should never see York."

"No," one of his companions corrected him, "she said you might see York, but never reach it."

Wolsey stared at the patchwork of fields, forest and moor that stretched beyond the clustering thatched roofs below. He did not move. But he knew the voice that spoke at his elbow.

"I vow," he said in a low voice, "that I'll have her burned when I get there. And I soon will be."

But then he turned and saw the man whose voice he knew. It was Lord Percy, Earl of Northumberland. "You have come for me," he said.

"Yes, my lord," said Lord Percy. "You are to travel south and face a charge of high treason."

The next day they began the journey back to London. At Leicester, Wolsey's illness became worse. The monks nursed him, but he never regained consciousness and there, a broken man, he died. Mother Shipton may have felt satisfied, but there were many who grieved, for Wolsey like many such larger-than-life men, had possessed great qualities as well as faults.

Such foreknowledge sealed Mother Shipton's reputation. During the years that followed her name became synonymous with dark warnings of the future. And the immediate future was more turbulent than ever, especially in Yorkshire.

But the King and Parliament crushed any rebellion. Among those who died were the Earl of Northumberland, Lord Percy, and his friend Lord D'Arcy; and they died on the pavements of York.

Henry VIII died not long afterwards on January 28 1547. He left a country profoundly changed from that which he had inherited less than 40 years before. The old power of the medieval church had been broken. Parliament had new authority.

Beech trees in Autumn

The Flax Mill Weir.

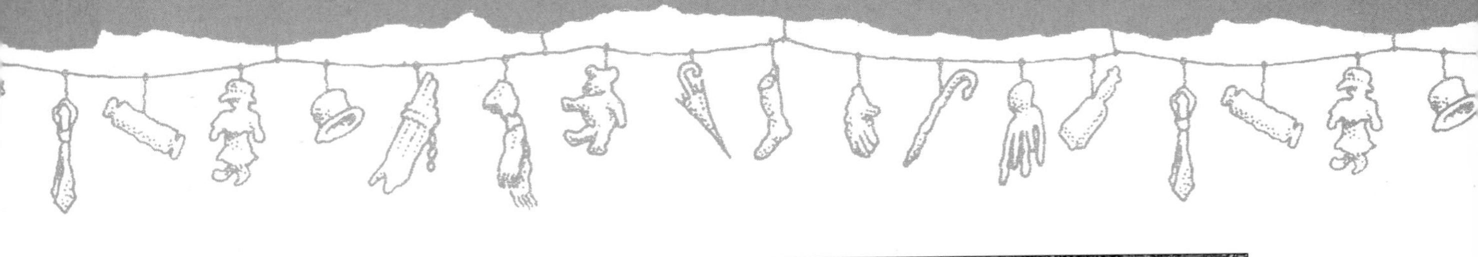

The Nidd Gorge

Woodland walk

He was succeeded by his only son, Edward VI, just nine years old. Mother Shipton's words echoed in the uneasy air.

"For a sweet pious Prince make room
And in each kirk prepare a broom
For this Prince that shall never be born
Shall make the shaven heads forlorn."

Edward VI was not born in the usual way but by a crude Caesarian operation which killed his mother, Jane Seymour. Her brother, the Duke of Somerset, was appointed Protector of England, to rule for the child King. The "shaven heads" – the tonsured monks – were certainly to be forlorn, since the conflict between the Catholic and Protestant churches was now increasing and the Protestants, for the time being, were in the ascendant.

"Then shall Commons rise in arms,
And women's malice cause much harm.
Oh deadly pride! Oh hateful strife!
Brothers to seek each other's life.
Ambition shall so deadly spread,
The Griffin fierce shall lose his head.
Soon after shall the Lion die,
And mildness usher cruelty."

The "Commons" – the ordinary people – did rise in arms, desperate to stop the rising anarchy in the country which threatened to engulf them. Inflation is a word we think belongs to our own time but it has always been the root of chaos. Prices were rocketing. The impoverished were becoming destitute. Landlords were enclosing what had been open common land on which the peasants had grown their crops and grazed their cattle and sheep.

"A virtuous Lady then shall die,
For being raised up so high –
Her death shall cause another's joy,
Who will the kingdom much annoy."

Castle Top and the Waterside

Cardinal Wolsey

Henry VIII

York Minster, 18 miles from Mother Shipton's Cave

The virtuous Lady Jane Grey, was the young and innocent victim of the struggle between those who believed Mary to be the rightful heir. Edward, still only a boy, died prematurely: Lady Jane was beheaded and Mary did become Queen of England. Mother Shipton calls her "Alecto", one of the Furies in Greek mythology. She lived up to her name. She was married to Prince Phillip of Spain and thus reinforced her already passionate Catholicism, encouraged by her new Archbishop of Canterbury, Reginald Pole, who was also a Cardinal of Rome.Now began such a period of barbaric persecution of Protestants with men, women and children often burned alive, that England rejected Catholicism as its national religion for ever.

"Alecto next assumes the crown;
And mitres shall rise, and heads fall down,
And streams of blood run Smithfield down.
England shall join in league with Spain,
Which some to hinder strive in vain.
Alecto then shall from Life retire,
And Pontifical Priest expire."

The blood did run in Smithfield for it was one of the places to burn martyrs. And when Mary Tudor died in the early morning of November 17 1558, it was only a few hours later on the same day that Cardinal Pole, her "Pontifical Priest", died too.

It was the end of an era. Nothing would ever be the same again for England; but at least the anarchy and bloodshed ceased. Where there had been conflict between those who professed the same God but not the same symbols there was a new tolerance. And much of the reason lay in the character of the new Queen on the throne of England. Elizabeth I was a girl of 25 when she came to rule. She was never to marry but she would reign for more than 45 years and bring peace and pride to her country. Though there would be war in her time, on this occasion the invading "wooden horses" of the great Spanish fleet would be destroyed by Sir Francis Drake and his nimble English men o' war.

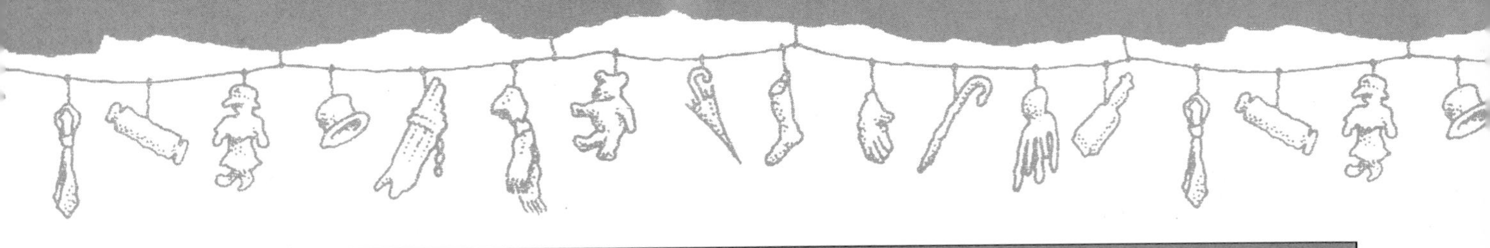

Micklegate Bar. The heads of the Duke of Northumberland and Lord D'Arcy were publicly displayed here.

"The maiden Queen full many a year
Shall England's warlike sceptre bear.
Those who sighed, then shall sing,
And the bells shall changes ring.
The Papal power shall bear no sway,
And Rome's trash shall hence be swept away.
The locusts from the Seven Hills
This English Rose shall seek to kill -
And the Western monarch's wooden horses
Shall be destroyed by Drake's forces."

Mother Shipton also speaks of the death of Mary, Queen of Scots, and the achievement of an uneasy peace in war-torn Ireland – just another of the curious parallels with our own time. In the same passage she refers to the beheading of the Earl of Essex. Elizabeth loved the arrogant, ambitious, fiery Essex but those very qualities made him her rival and in the end she agreed to his death. She was nearly 70 years old but she still loved him and she must have been tortured by what she felt she had to do. It was not long after Essex's death that Elizabeth herself died, a lonely figure at the end.

"A Widowed Queen (Mary, Queen of Scots)
In England shall be headless seen.
The Harp (Ireland) shall give a better sound,
An Earl without a Head be found.
Soon after shall the English Rose
Unto a Male her place dispose."

James VI of Scotland inherited the English crown from Elizabeth, when she died in 1603. Janus, to whom Mother Shipton refers in her prophecy, was the Greek god of two faces who presided over gates, doorways – and new beginnings. His temple in Rome was shut only in times of peace. And this time a King of Scotland crossed the River Tweed not to die upon a Northumberland field but to ride on to London and thus unite the two ancient enemies.

"The northern line of Tweed
The maiden Queen shall next succeed
And join in one, two, mighty States
- then shall Janus shut his gates."

Mother Shipton died at the beginning of Queen Elizabeth I's long reign. It is said that she predicted her own death in 1561. Perhaps it was a fitting moment. In her own way Ursula Shipton had been a part of the turbulent age which had seen so much great change in England. Her voice had been heard in the highest places in the land, sometimes as a warning, sometimes as a kind of commentary, throughout those dark years of conflict.

She was buried, it is said, in unconsecrated ground somewhere on the outskirts of York. Rumours of her links with the spirit world lasted to the end. By tradition a stone was raised on her grave with the following inscription:

"Here lies she who never lied,
Whose skill so often has been tried
Her prophecies shall still survive
And ever keep her name alive."

The stone, said to have been removed at some time to a museum in York, has now disappeared.

Yet her name persists. In the years after her death people still interpreted her prophecies, according to their own age. When Charles I was beheaded and England ruled by the Lord Protector Oliver Cromwell, people recalled her words.

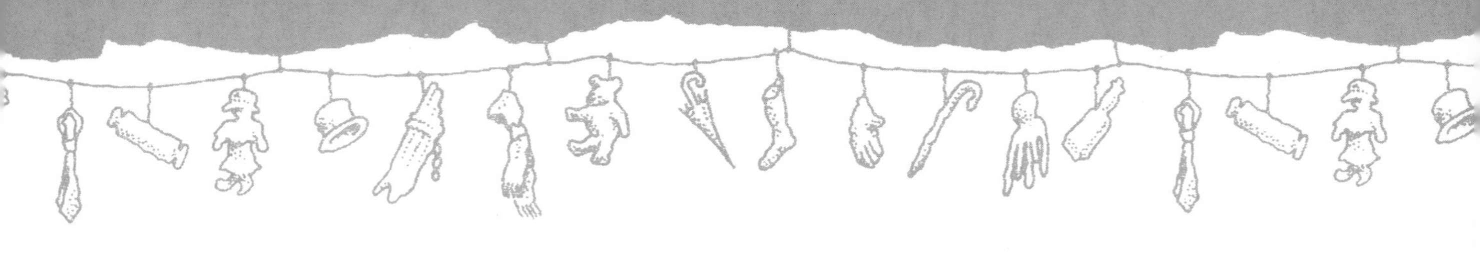

The Petrifying Well

Parish Church and the Old Manor House

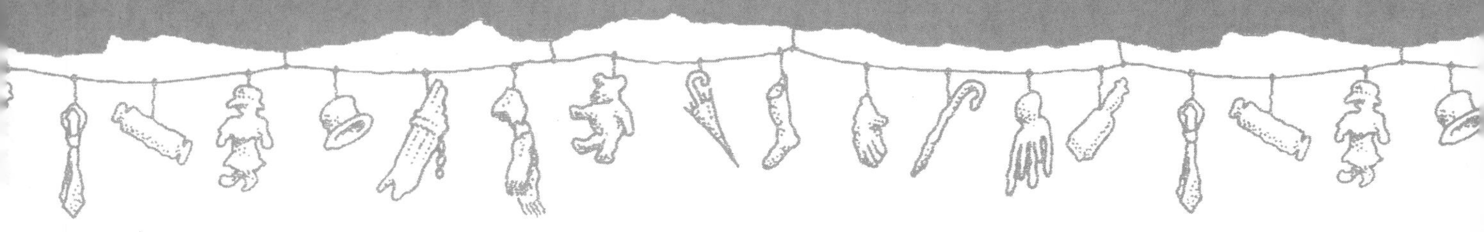

"The White King dead, the Wolf shall then
With blood usurp the lion's den."

In 1665 the Great Plague ravaged London and there was talk of Mother Shipton's image: "Triumphant death rides London through". A year later the Great Fire of London started in Pudding Lane and Samuel Pepys recorded in his Diary: "See – Mother Shipton's word is out." For she had foretold that the houses of London would fall and men walk upon their rooftops and that a ship should sail up the Thames and find a ruined city so that its Master would weep and lament the city he remembered and that scarcely a house was left to provide a flagon of wine.

Then there was the long passage of strange images which may or may not be Mother Shipton's own words and which seems to have curious relevance to our own time. Some of them seem to have been fulfilled; some remain mysterious. Perhaps you will understand them.

"The fiery year as soon as O'er,
Peace shall then be as before;
Plenty everywhere be found,
And men with swords shall plough the ground.
The time shall come when seas of blood
Shall mingle with a greater flood.
Carriages without horses shall go.
And accidents fill the world with woe.

Around the world thoughts shall fly
In the twinkling of an eye.

Waters shall yet more wonders do,
How strange yet shall be true.
The world upside down shall be,
And gold found at the root of a tree.

Through hills men shall ride
And no horse or ass be by their side;
Under water men shall walk,
Shall ride, shall sleep, shall talk;
In the air men shall be seen,
In white, in black and in green.

Iron in the water shall float
As easy as a wooden boat;
Gold shall be found, and found,
In a land that's not now known.
Fire and water shall more wonders do
England shall at last admit a Jew;
The Jew that was held in scorn
Shall of a Christian be born and born.

A house of glass shall come to pass
In England, but alas!
War will follow with the work
In the land of the Pagan and Turk
And state and state in fierce strife
Will seek each other's life
But when the North shall divide the South
An eagle shall build in the lion's mouth.

An Ape shall appear in a Leap year
That shall put all womankind in fear
And Adam's make shall be disputed
And Roman faith shall like rooted
And England will turn around.

Thunder shall shake the earth;
Lightning shall rend asunder;
Water shall fill the earth
Fire shall do its work.

Three times shall lovely France
Be led to dance a bloody dance;
Before her people shall be free.
Three tyrant rulers shall she see;
Three times the People rule alone;
Three times the People's hope is gone;
Three rulers in succession see,
Each spring from different dynasty.
Then shall the worser fight be done,
England and France shall be as one.

Waters shall flow where corn shall grow
Corn shall grow where waters doth flow
Houses shall appear in the vales below
And covered by hail and snow;
White shall be black, then turn grey
And a fair lady be married thrice.

All England's sons that plough the land
Shall be seen, book in hand;
Learning shall so ebb and flow,
The poor shall most wisdom know."

It is possible that these passages are from a 19th century fabrication and certainly the style has a rather modern ring to it. But another of Mother Shipton's prophecies recorded much earlier has its own strange beauty of imagery. It is perhaps the most enigmatic of them all.

"The lily shall remain in a merry world; and he shall be moved against the seed of the lion, and shall stand on one side of the country with a number of ships. Then shall the Son of Man, having a fierce beast in his arms, whose Kingdom is the land of the moon, which is dreaded throughout the world. With a number shall he pass many waters and shall come to the land of the lion, looking for help from the beast of his country, and an eagle shall come out of the east, spread with the beams of the Son of Man, and shall destroy castles of the Thames. And there shall be battles among many kingdoms. That year shall be the bloody field, and lily F.K shall lose his crown, and therewith be crowned the Son of Man K.W and the fourth year shall be preferred. And there shall be a universal peace over the whole world, and there shall be plenty of fruits; and then he shall go to the land of the Cross."

What must be certain is that some 500 years ago a woman called Mistress Shipton lived here in Knaresborough and that when she spoke people believed her and passed her words on. Did she live somewhere near the Petrifying Well, where the strange little stream with its powers to turn to stone ran down into the River Nidd? Perhaps she walked here along what is now called The Long Walk, gathering herbs for her potions and healing remedies. Here in the cool quiet she could listen to the song of birds and sit upon a mossy stone to let the wild creatures approach. They were never cruel; they did not mock her. I think she must have been a remarkable woman, and I hope that her shade, wherever it lingers, is grateful for some understanding.

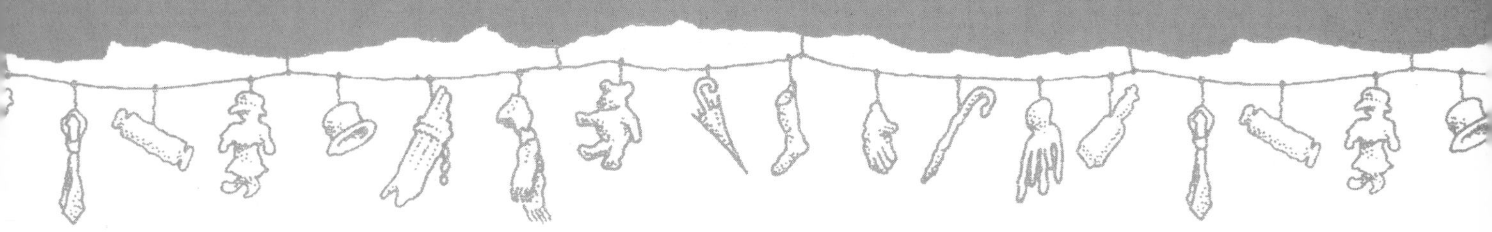

The Petrifying Well

Over the years millions of people have come to see for themselves the amazing powers of the Petrifying Well.

This ancient well – formerly known as the Dropping Well – is believed to be the only one of its kind in England and it first went on public display in 1630. Ever since people have flocked to witness the water turning objects to stone before their very eyes.

For centuries the Petrifying Well was shrouded in mystery and superstition. Leaves, birds and small animals which tumbled in were gradually coated with a hard layer of rock – and so the rumours of witchcraft and magic spread.

The Petrifying Well water eventually became known for its health-giving properties and back in the early 1600s it had been examined and deemed a miracle cure for any "Flux of the Body"! But it is only in the last 150 years that scientific analysis has revealed exactly what lies behind the "magical" petrification process.

For the geologists among you here are some hard facts! The water springs from an underground lake and seeps through the earth's crust via a layer of rock called an "aquifer".

The spring has never been known to dry up and an estimated 700 gallons of water flow through the well every hour summer and winter, in drought or flood.

Its high mineral content means everything porous in its path is turned to stone. Over a period of months and years the water leaves behind mineral deposits which build up to form a crust of new rock.

The minerals most abundantly present are calcium, sodium and magnesium, with traces of lead, zinc, iron, manganese and aluminium. These exist mainly in the form of sulphates and carbonates with some chlorides and a little silica. The proportions have remained more or less regular over many years.

As the water emerges into the atmosphere calcite (calcium carbonate) is deposited along with small amounts of other minerals and over the years this builds up a crust of new rock.

Twice in the recent past this has led to the collapse of the well itself. Huge sections broke away in 1816 and then in 1821. But there is no danger of a similar incident today. The well face is scraped with wire brushes every six weeks and this painstaking job means it should never become too top-heavy.

The appearance and texture of the new rock depends on how quickly the minerals are formed and hence the size of their crystals.

Tufa is a soft, porous rock with microscopic crystals. This is the quickest forming deposit of the Petrifying Well and grows where a constant flow of air causes rapid evaporation and cooling of the water.

Travertine is harder and more compact, forming where water trickles slowly over a broad area. Crystals grow continually upwards at right angles to the surface in a solid mass.

At different times of the year the mineral content of the water varies very slightly and this results in the dark and light coloured bands. Travertine can cut and polished and is a suitable stone for jewellery.

The two types of deposit can merge and the travertine often covers a mass of tufa which has cemented together debris like dead vegetation or fragmented rock.

The Victorian Railway Viaduct crosses Mother Shipton's Historic Park and the Nidd Gorge.

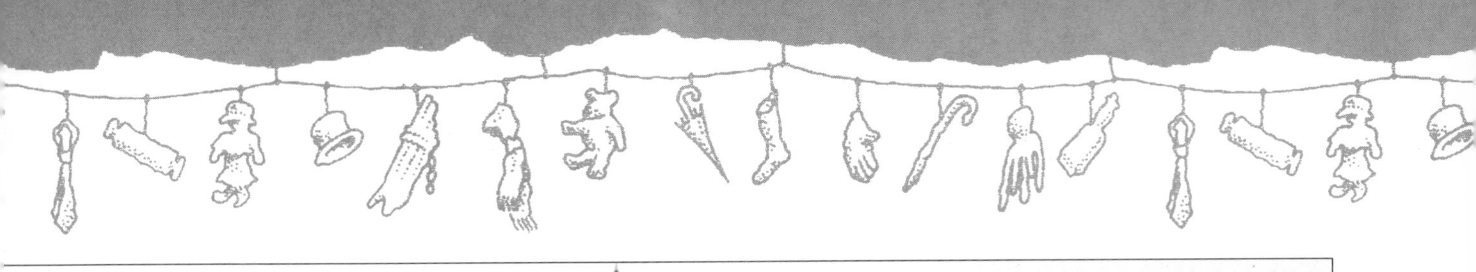

Two large bumps are clearly visible jutting out from the rock face of the Petrifying Well. These are a gentleman's hat and a lady's bonnet placed there by a couple on their way to York Races in 1853. For some unknown reason they never returned to collect them and they show clearly the accumulation of rock in almost 150 years – notwithstanding the scraping!

Modern day visitors to the Petrifying Well see a whole host of everyday objects slowly being petrified in the cascading water. The most popular items are teddy bears and other small cuddly toys which usually take up to six months to turn to stone. Larger articles can take anything up to 18 months.

Many celebrities have donated items to be petrified here – and even a member of the Royal family has succumbed to the magic of the well.

Queen Mary, who came to see the Cave and Well in August 1923, left behind a shoe for petrification. It now takes pride of place in the Historia Museum.

The nation's favourite television soap stars have also been amazed by the Petrifying Well. Emmerdale characters Jack and Pat Sugden were shown on screen visiting Mother Shipton's Cave on their honeymoon and they left behind the bridal bouquet to be petrified.

Visitors can see a camisole sent by the country's most famous pub landlady – Coronation Street's Bet Gilroy – and a pair of high-heeled shoes once worn in the Rovers Return by barmaid Racquel are still hanging in the well undergoing the petrification process.

The Petrifying Well also conjured up a special gift for Sir Peter Wright CBE, former director of the Birmingham Royal Ballet. Ballerina Marion Tait OBE approached Mother Shipton's Cave about helping her create a unique gift for him on his retirement.

A pair of her tiny pink ballet shoes were hung in the water and turned to stone just in time to be presented to Sir Peter at a gala dinner last year.

It seems the petrification process may no longer be a mystery – but it's still "magic"!

Ferry to Dropping Well, Knaresborough.

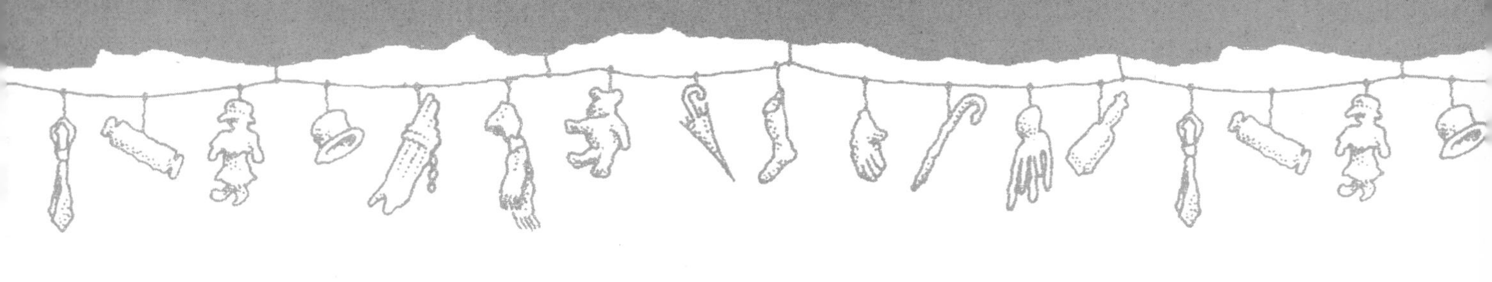

The Petrifying Well on a Winter's day.

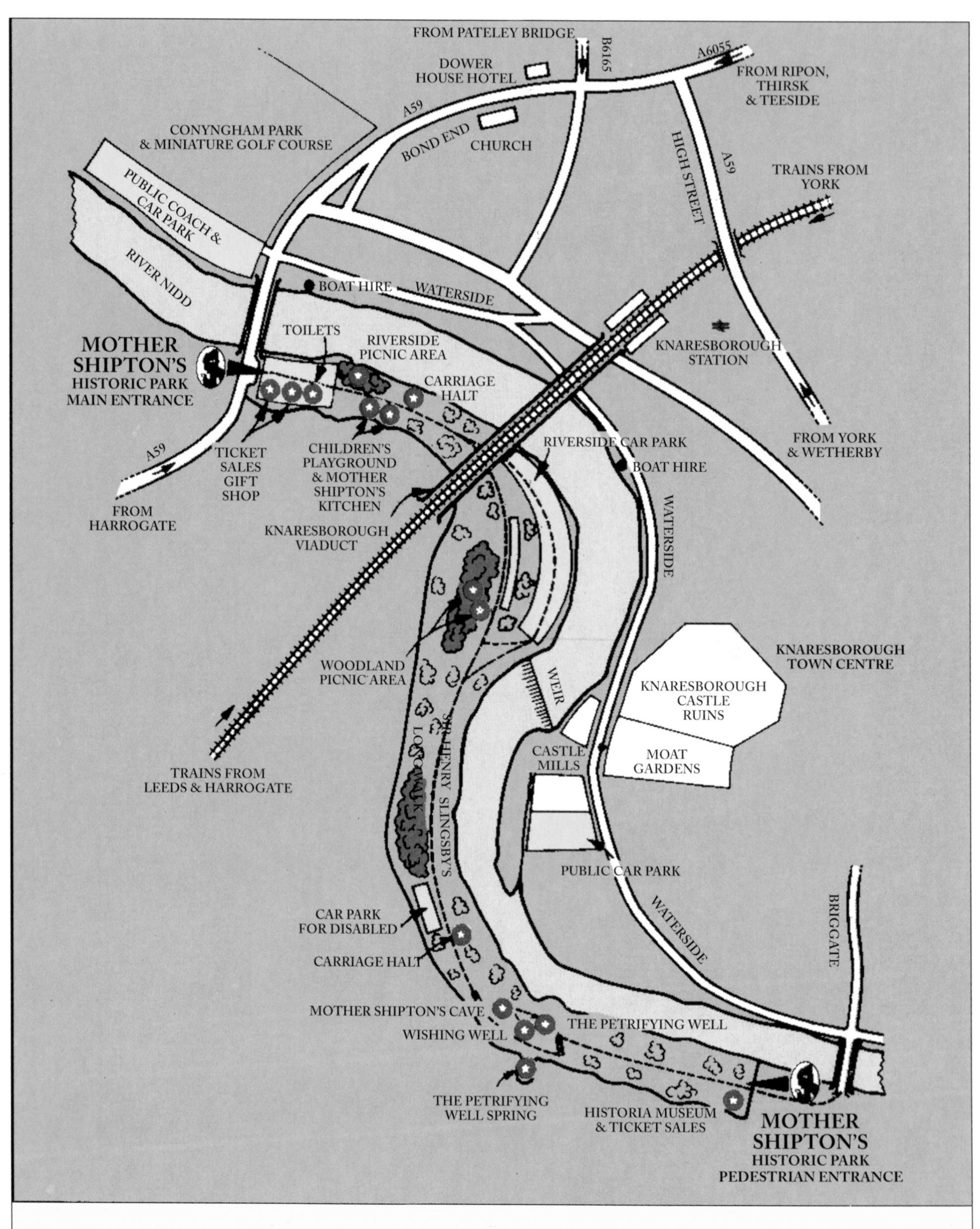

Written by Diana Windsor
Photography by Unichrome Ltd, Ian Wolverson
Published by Mother Shipton's Cave (Ilex Leisure Ltd)